Picture Clu[es]
ABC Names

JoAnn Johnson
Illustrated by Brad Bamba

ISBN 13: 978-1-59298-965-2

Library of Congress Catalog Number: 2013916180

Printed in the United States of America

First Printing: 2014

17 16 15 14 13 5 4 3 2 1

Cover design by Laura Drew
Cover and interior illustration © Brad Bamba

Beaver's Pond Press
7108 Ohms Lane
Edina, MN 55439–2129
952-829-8818

To order, visit www.BeaversPondBooks.com
or call 1-800-901-3480. Reseller discounts available.

ABOUT THIS BOOK

The purpose of this book is to teach letter names of the English alphabet using picture clues. The reasons to use this approach, based on my thirty-five years in teaching, are numerous.

- Learning letter name only can be less confusing than learning letter name and sound at the same time.

- Visual clues make learning faster and easier. Letter shapes are embedded into the picture. (Notice how the letter J is shaped like a worm for the jay.)

- Listening for sounds in words helps with reading and spelling.

- Tracing the letter will help those who learn through touch and motion.

Although the picture clues are of lowercase letters, the transfer to uppercase letters will be easy once the letter name concept is understood.

HOW TO USE THIS BOOK

Look at the letters at the top of the page.

If the person does not know the letter name:
1. Ask, "What is the clue?" The clue is the first line below the picture.
The sentences are just added reinforcement.
2. Ask, "What do you hear at the beginning of…"

Example 1: Letter Name "a"
If the person does not know the letter name "a":
1. Ask, "What is the clue?" The person should answer "acorn."
2. Ask, "What do you hear at the beginning of acorn?"
The person should answer "a."

acorn
The squirrel loves the big acorn.

Example 2: Letter Name "c"
If the person does not know the letter name "c":
1. Ask, "What is the clue?" The person should answer "seal."
2. Ask, "What do you hear at the beginning of seal?"
The person should answer "c."

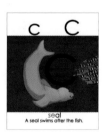

seal
A seal swims after the fish.

Don't be concerned about the spelling of the clue word.
The goal is to listen to sounds in the clues.

For learners having difficulty with this skill, introduce just one or two letters at a time, and as the names are learned, add another letter.

UPPERCASE LETTERS:

A B C D
E F G H
I J K L
M N O P
Q R S T
U V W X
Y Z

lowercase letters:

a b c d

e f g h

i j k l

m n o p

q r s t

u v w x

y z

a   A

acorn

The squirrel loves the big acorn.

b   B

bee

The bee likes flowers to make honey.

c C

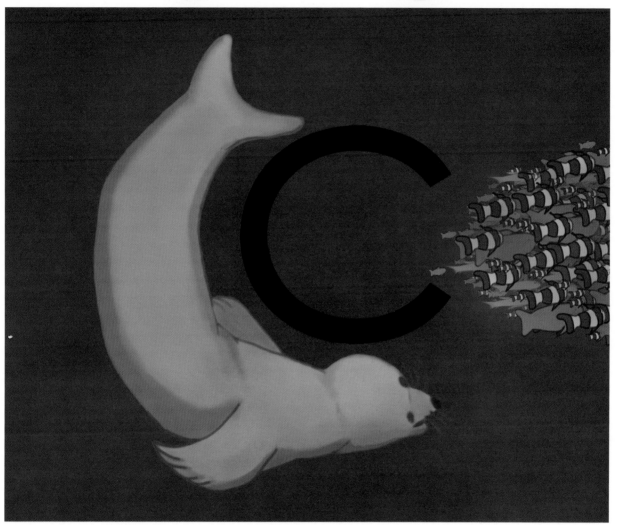

C

seal

The seal swims after the fish.

d   D

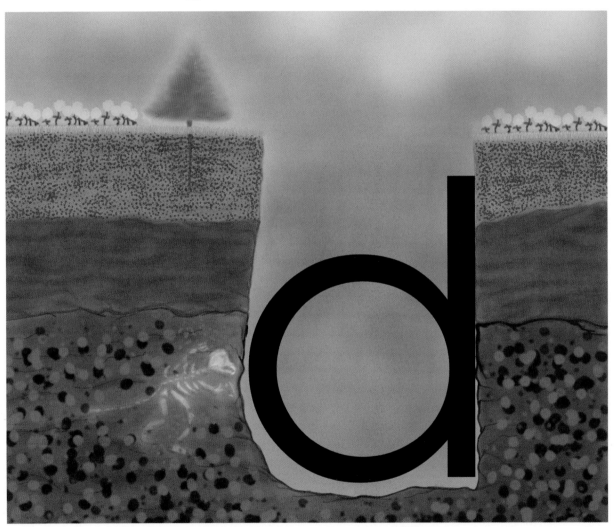

deep hole

That is a deep hole!

e E

eagle

An eagle is hatching an egg.

f   F

effort

It takes effort to run uphill.

g   G

jeans

Jeans are drying in the breeze.

h   H

ate cheese

The mouse ate cheese.

i   I

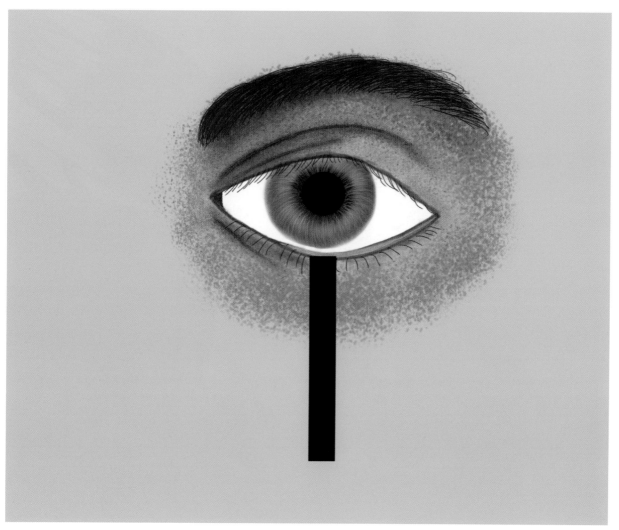

eye

Look into my eye.

j J

jay

The blue jay is catching a worm.

k K

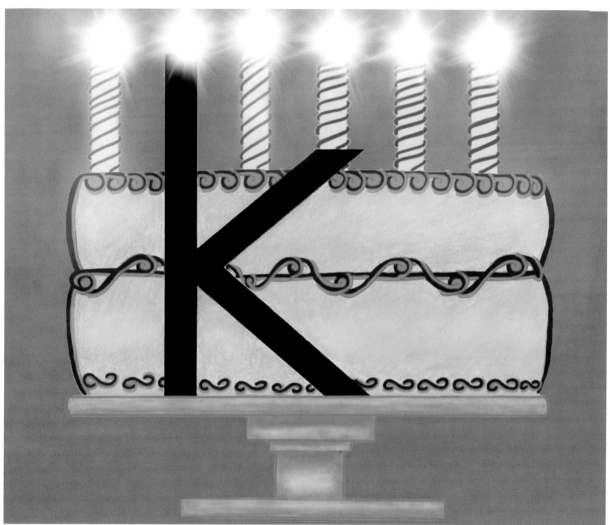

cake

Is this cake for a birthday party?

I L

elephant

An elephant does a trick.

m   M

empty

Empty the bags into the trash can.

n   N

enter

The bears enter the cave.

ocean

The sun shines over the ocean.

p P

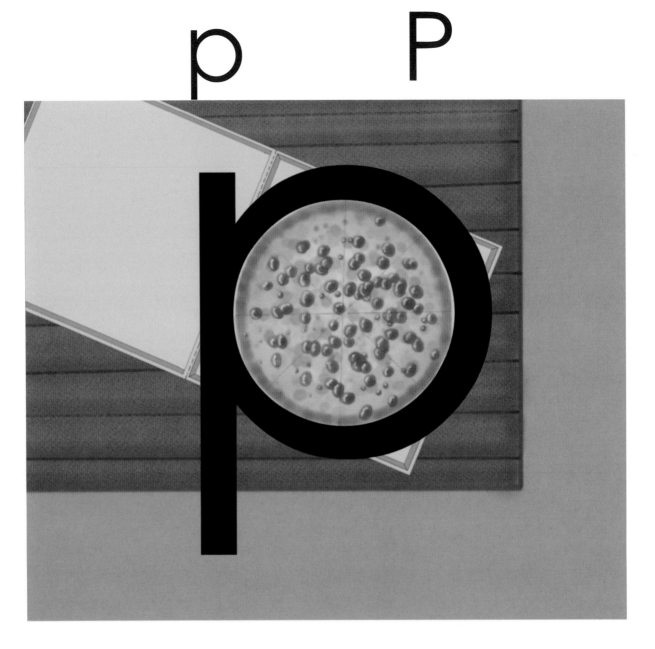

p

pizza

Do you like pizza?

q Q

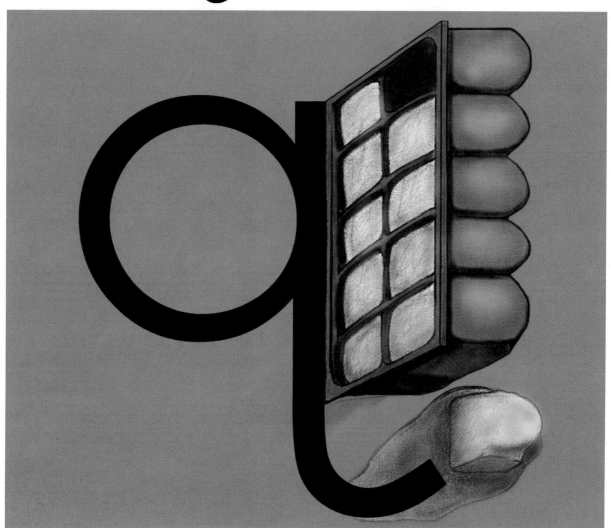

cube

The ice cube is melting.

r R

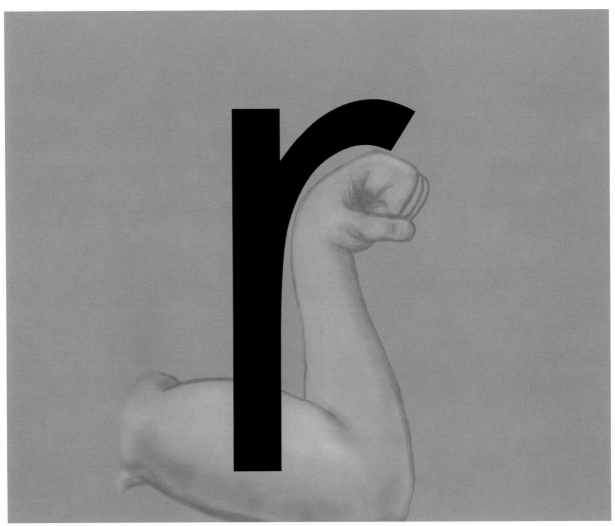

arm

This arm is strong.

s S

S

escalator

The girl rides the escalator.

† T

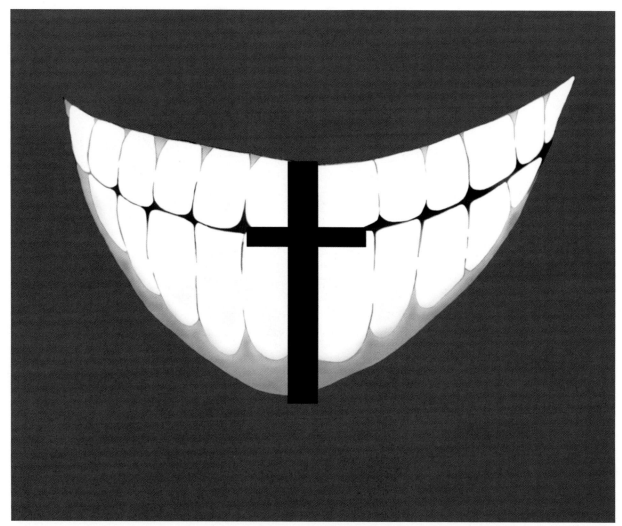

teeth

Teeth need to be brushed every day.

u U

u

unicorn

A unicorn has one horn on its head.

v V

vehicles on TV

Many vehicles are on TV.

double dip for you

Here are double dip cones for you!

X X

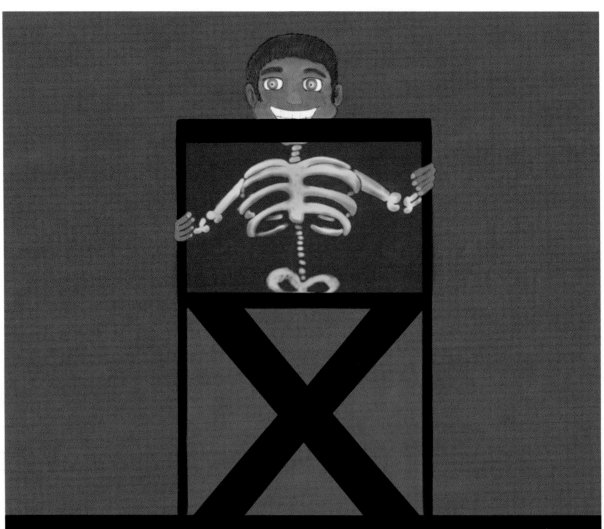

x-ray

An x-ray can show your bones.

y Y

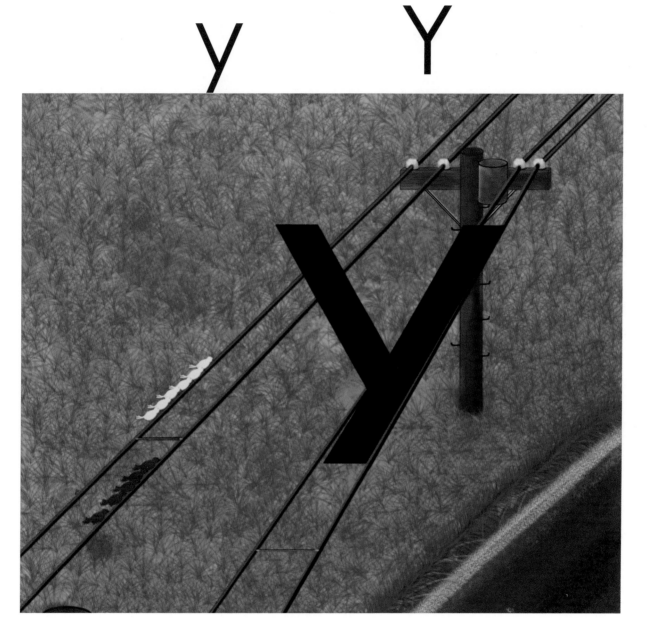

Y

wire

The birds are sitting on a wire.

zebra

The zebra likes to eat grass.